WHAT ARE INVASIVE SPECIES?

THERESA EMMINIZER

T0002040

Enslow
PUBLISHING

Please visit our website, www.enslow.com.
For a free color catalog of all our high-quality books, call toll free
1-800-398-2504 or fax 1-877-980-4454.

Library of Congress Cataloging-in-Publication Data
Names: Emminizer, Theresa, author.
Title: What are invasive species? / Theresa Emminizer.
Description: Buffalo, New York : Enslow Publishing, [2023] | Series: Eye on
   ecosystems | Includes index. | Summary: "Originally native to the
   Caspian and Black Seas, zebra mussels are now widespread throughout the
   United States. Transported accidentally, these quickly reproducing
   creatures soon became a deadly invasive species. From zebra mussels to
   water hyacinths, invasive species are wreaking havoc on many ecosystems.
   In this accessible and informative book, young readers will learn about
   the dangers of invasive species, how they harm habitats, and what can be
   done about it. Real-world examples, simple language, and colorful
   photographs bring key science concepts to life for developing minds"–
   Provided by publisher.
Identifiers: LCCN 2022024443 (print) | LCCN 2022024444 (ebook) | ISBN
   9781978532694 (library binding) | ISBN 9781978532670 (paperback) | ISBN
   9781978532700 (ebook)
Subjects: LCSH: Introduced organisms–Juvenile literature.
Classification: LCC QH353 .E46 2023 (print) | LCC QH353 (ebook) | DDC
   578.6/2–dc23/eng/20220623
LC record available at https://lccn.loc.gov/2022024443
LC ebook record available at https://lccn.loc.gov/2022024444

Published in 2023 by
Enslow Publishing
2544 Clinton Street
Buffalo, NY 14224

Designer: Tanya Dellaccio
Editor: Theresa Emminizer

Photo credits: Cover ervision Creative/Shutterstock.com; p. 5 Kurit afshen/Shutterstock.com; p. 6 Gina Santoria/Shutterstock.com; p. 7 Ger
Bosma Photos/Shutterstock.com; p. 9 bearacreative/Shutterstock.com; p. 10 1082492116/Shutterstock.com; p. 11 Jeff Caughey/Shutterstock.
com; p. 13 Heiko Kiera/Shutterstock.com; p. 15 Ondrej Prosicky/Shutterstock.com; p. 16 EKramar/Shutterstock.com; p. 17 Tatevosian Yana/
Shutterstock.com; p. 19 Ronnachai Palas/Shutterstock.com; p. 21 Sergey Novikov/Shutterstock.com.

CPSIA compliance information: Batch #CWENS23: For further information contact Enslow Publishing at 1-800-398-2504.

Find us on

CONTENTS

Boldface words appear in Words to Know.

WHAT'S AN INVASIVE SPECIES?

An ecosystem is a natural community of living and nonliving things. When an organism, or living thing, that's not native to the ecosystem moves in, it can become an invasive species. Invasive species can cause a lot of harm.

DIFFERENT SPECIES, OR KINDS, OF ORGANISMS **INTERACT** IN AN ECOSYSTEM.

Not all non-native species are invasive. To be invasive, a species must easily adapt, or change, to suit its new **environment**. It must reproduce, or have babies, quickly. It must be harmful to the native environment and things that live there.

THE ASIAN
LADY
BEETLE IS
AN INVASIVE
SPECIES.

WHY ARE THEY HARMFUL?

Invasive species **compete** with native species for food and other **resources**. They may change the environment in ways that make it harder for native species to survive, or live. They can even drive native species to **extinction**!

INVASIVE LIONFISH PUT NATIVE FISH IN DANGER.

HOW DO THEY SPREAD?

Invasive species are introduced, or brought into, ecosystems in different ways. Most are by mistake! Sometimes invasive species are carried on boats or on firewood. Other times they're introduced when people release, or let out, non-native pets.

INVASIVE ZEBRA MUSSELS SPREAD TO THE UNITED STATES ON SHIPS.

PYTHONS IN THE EVERGLADES

Burmese pythons are big snakes that are native to Southeast Asia. They were brought to the United States as pets. Some pythons escaped or were released by their owners and have spread throughout the Florida Everglades. They prey on, or eat, native birds and **mammals**.

PYTHONS HAVE FEW NATURAL **PREDATORS** IN THE EVERGLADES.

CANE TOADS IN AUSTRALIA

Some invasive species were introduced on purpose. During the 1930s, people brought South American cane toads to Australia. Farmers hoped they'd eat cane beetles, which were harming their crops. Instead, cane toads spread out of control, becoming a deadly invasive species.

CANE TOADS ARE **POISONOUS** AND CAN KILL MANY NATIVE CREATURES.

CONTROLLING INVASIVE SPECIES

The best way to control invasive species is to prevent, or stop, them from spreading in the first place! Otherwise, they must be eradicated, or removed by force. Replanting or bringing back native species while removing invasive ones helps **restore** the ecosystem.

LEARNING ABOUT NATIVE SPECIES IS A GREAT WAY TO HELP THE ENVIRONMENT!

WHAT CAN YOU DO?

An important way to help keep native plants and animals safe is to keep your pets (especially cats) indoors. Never release a pet into the wild. Even small creatures like rabbits and fish can be very harmful when introduced to natural ecosystems.

STAYING HOME KEEPS YOUR PET SAFE AND KEEPS LOCAL ANIMALS SAFE TOO!

19

Wipe off your shoes before and after you go hiking in a new area! This clears off any seeds or bugs that might be invasive. If you're out **exploring**, don't take home any non-native plants, animals, shells, or wood that you might find.

YOU CAN HELP **PROTECT** THE ENVIRONMENT!

WORDS TO KNOW

compete: To try to gain something before another does.

environment: The natural place where a plant or animal lives.

explore: To search in order to find new things.

extinction: The death of all members of a species.

interact: To act upon one another.

mammal: A warm-blooded animal that has a backbone and hair, breathes air, and feeds milk to its young.

poisonous: Having poison, a harmful matter that can cause illness or death.

predator: An animal that hunts other animals for food.

protect: To keep safe.

resource: Something that can be used.

restore: To bring back.

FOR MORE INFORMATION

BOOKS

Hames, Rachael. *Loss of Biodiversity*. New York, NY: PowerKids Press, 2018.

Regan, Lisa. *Habitats*. New York, NY: PowerKids Press, 2020.

WEBSITES

eek! Environmental Education for Kids

www.eekwi.org/alien-invaders

Learn how to spot non-native species.

National Institute of Environmental Health Services

kids.niehs.nih.gov/topics/natural-world/wildlife/invasives/index.html

Learn more about invasive species and how to stop them.

INDEX